Mel Bay Presents

Songs of **MEXIC** **FOR ACCORDION**

by Herman Troppe

1 2 3 4 5 6 7 8 9 0

© 2000 BY MEL BAY PUBLICATIONS, INC., PACIFIC, MO 63069.
ALL RIGHTS RESERVED. INTERNATIONAL COPYRIGHT SECURED. B.M.I. MADE AND PRINTED IN U.S.A.
No part of this publication may be reproduced in whole or in part, or stored in a retrieval system, or transmitted in any form
or by any means, electronic, mechanical, photocopy, recording, or otherwise, without written permission of the publisher.

Visit us on the Web at www.melbay.com — E-mail us at email@melbay.com

Table of Contents

Hay Unos Ojos
There Are Some Eyes

Arr. © 1998 Mel Bay Publications, Inc.
All Rights Reserved. International Copyright Secured.

La Malagueña

Arr. © 1998 Mel Bay Publications, Inc.
All Rights Reserved. International Copyright Secured.

Cielito Lindo (I)
Beautiful Heaven

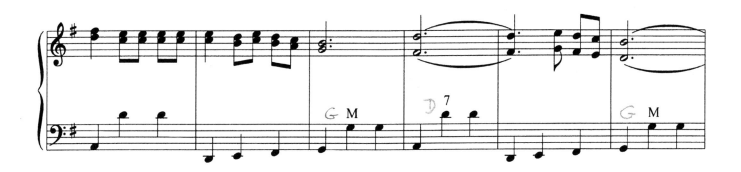

Arr. © 1998 Mel Bay Publications, Inc.
All Rights Reserved. International Copyright Secured.

Cielito Lindo (II)
Beautiful Heaven

Arr. © 1998 Mel Bay Publications, Inc.
All Rights Reserved. International Copyright Secured.

Chiapanecas

Arr. © 1998 Mel Bay Publications, Inc.
All Rights Reserved. International Copyright Secured.

Rifaré Mi Suerte
I Will Raffle My Future

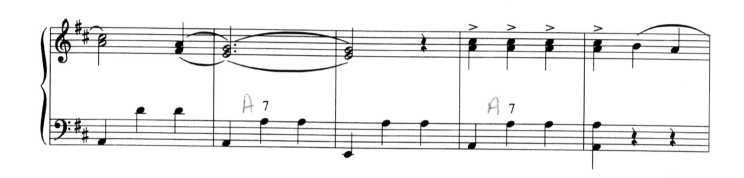

Arr. © 1998 Mel Bay Publications, Inc.
All Rights Reserved. International Copyright Secured.

13

La Zandunga

Arr. © 1998 Mel Bay Publications, Inc.
All Rights Reserved. International Copyright Secured.

Roman Castillo

Arr. © 1998 Mel Bay Publications, Inc.
All Rights Reserved. International Copyright Secured.

La Bamba

Arr. © 1998 Mel Bay Publications, Inc.
All Rights Reserved. International Copyright Secured.

Las Mañanitas
Morning Greetings
Birthday Song

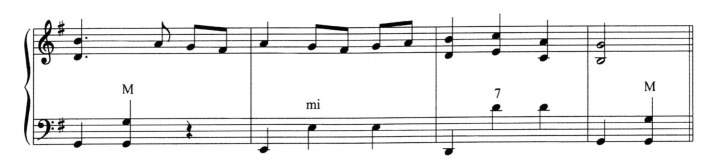

Arr. © 1998 Mel Bay Publications, Inc.
All Rights Reserved. International Copyright Secured.

El Abandonado
The Abandoned One

Arr. © 1998 Mel Bay Publications, Inc.
All Rights Reserved. International Copyright Secured.

Desede México He Venido
Mexico Is Where I've Come From

Arr. © 1998 Mel Bay Publications, Inc.
All Rights Reserved. International Copyright Secured.

De Colores
Brilliant Colors

Arr. © 1998 Mel Bay Publications, Inc.
All Rights Reserved. International Copyright Secured.

Los Braceros
The Migratory Workers

Benito Amado
Justine Alares

Arr. © 1998 Mel Bay Publications, Inc.
All Rights Reserved. International Copyright Secured.

La Llorona
The Weeping One

Arr. © 1998 Mel Bay Publications, Inc.
All Rights Reserved. International Copyright Secured.

El Cascabel
The Little Bell

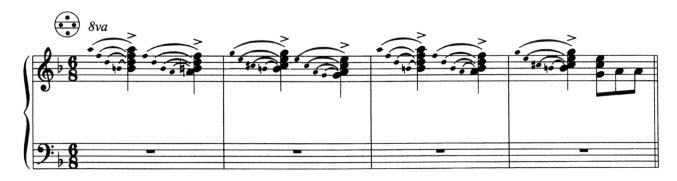

Arr. © 1998 Mel Bay Publications, Inc.
All Rights Reserved. International Copyright Secured.

Chorus

El Caballo Bayo
The Bay Horse

Arr. © 1998 Mel Bay Publications, Inc.
All Rights Reserved. International Copyright Secured.

Adios del Soldado
The Soldiers Farewell

Arr. © 1998 Mel Bay Publications, Inc.
All Rights Reserved. International Copyright Secured.

La Adelita

Arr. © 1998 Mel Bay Publications, Inc.
All Rights Reserved. International Copyright Secured.